Calling Time

Short plays
Derek Webb

New Theatre Publications - London
www.plays4theatre.com

2

© 2013 BY Derek Webb
First published in 2011

The edition published in 2013

New Theatre Publications

2 Hereford Close | Warrington | Cheshire | WA1 4HR | 01925 485605

www.plays4theatre.com   email: info@plays4theatre.com

New Theatre Publications is the trading name of the publishing house that is owned by members of the Playwrights' Co-operative. This innovative project was launched on the 1st October 1997 by writers Paul Beard and Ian Hornby with the aim of encouraging the writing and promotion of the very best in New Theatre by Professional and Amateur writers for the Professional and Amateur Theatre at home and abroad.

Rights of performance for NTP plays are controlled by New Theatre Publications, 2 Hereford Close, Warrington, Cheshire, WA1 4HR who will issue a performing licence on payment of a fee and subject to a number of conditions. These plays are fully protected under the Copyright Laws of the British Commonwealth of Nations, the United States of America and all countries of the Berne and Universal Copyright Conventions. All rights, including stage, motion picture, radio, television, public reading and translation into foreign languages are strictly reserved. It is an infringement of the copyright to give any performance or public reading of these plays before the fee has been paid and the licence issued. The royalty fee is subject to contract and subject to variation at the sole discretion of New Theatre Publications. In territories overseas the fees quoted in this catalogue may not apply. A fee will be quoted on application to New Theatre Publications.

The right of Derek Webb to be identified as author of this work has been asserted by him in accordance with Section 77 of the Copyright, Designs and Patents Act 1988

ISBN 9 781 840 94923 0

Characters

Woman 1 - Caroline, Kathy, Tracy
Man 1 - Bill, Adrian, Simon
Woman 2 - Janine, Emma, Rebecca
Man 2 - Paul, Tim, Joe

Copyright Information

The play is fully protected under the Copyright laws of the British Commonwealth of Nations, the United States of America and all countries of the Berne and Universal Copyright Conventions.

All rights including Stage, Motion Picture, Radio, television, Public Reading, and Translation into Foreign Languages, are strictly reserved.

No part of this publication may lawfully be reproduced in ANY form or by any means - photocopying, typescript, recording (including video-recording), manuscript, electronic, mechanical or otherwise - or be transmitted or stored in a retrieval system, without prior permission.

Licenses for amateur performances are issued subject to the understanding that it shall be made clear in all advertising matter that the audience will witness an amateur performance; that the names of the authors of the plays shall be included on all programmes, and that the integrity of the authors' work will be preserved.

The Royalty Fee is subject to contract and subject to variation at the sole discretion of New Theatre Publications.

In Theatres of Halls seating Four Hundred or more the fee will be subject to negotiation.

In Territories Overseas the fee quoted may not apply. A fee will be quoted on application to New Theatre Publications, London.

Video-Recording of Amateur Productions

Please note that the copyright laws governing video-recording are extremely complex and that it should not be assumed that any play may be video-recorded for whatever purpose without first obtaining the permission of the appropriate agents. The fact that a play is published by New Theatre Publications does not indicate that video rights are available or that New Theatre Publications control such rights.

Performing Licence Applications

A performing licence for these plays will be issued by "New Theatre Publications" subject to the following conditions.

Conditions

1. That the performance fee is paid in full on the date of application for a licence.
2. That the name of the author(s) is/are clearly shown in any programme or publicity material.
3. That the author(s) is/are entitled to receive two complimentary tickets to see his/her/their work in performance if they so wish.
4. That a copy of the play is purchased from New Theatre Publications for each named speaking part and a minimum of three copies purchased for backstage use.
5. That a copy of any review be forwarded to New Theatre Publications.
6. That the New Theatre Publications logo is clearly shown on any publicity material. This is available on our website.

Fees

Details of script prices and fees payable for each performance or public reading can be obtained by telephone to (+44) 01925 485605 or to the address below.

Alternatively, latest prices can be obtained from our website www.plays4theatre.com where credit/debit cards can be used for payment.

To apply for a performing licence for any play please write to New Theatre Publications 2 Hereford Close, Warrington, Cheshire WA1 4HR or email info@plays4theatre.com with the following details:-

1. Name and address of theatre company.
2. Details of venue including seating capacity.
3. Dates of proposed performance or public reading.
4. Contact telephone number for Author's complimentary tickets.

Or apply directly via our website at www.plays4theatre.com

Calling Time
Five short linked black comedies set in a pub
by Derek Webb

The five scenes which make up 'Calling Time' are linked by situation and theme, but each one is separate in itself and the characters who appear in each do not appear in the others. The play is opened and closed with two short sequences which act as 'bookends', however it is possible to discard some of the intervening scenes to shorten the whole play accordingly if required, bearing in mind the time needed for costume changes etc. Similarly, while there are 12 parts in total, the piece allows great flexibility in casting. And all twelve parts can, with doubling and trebling, be played by a cast of two men and two women having playing age ranges from 20 to 50 as follows:-

Woman 1........................ *Caroline, Kathy, Tracy*
Man 1............................. *Bill, Adrian, Simon*
Woman 2..................... *Janine, Emma, Rebecca*
Man 2................................ *Paul, Tim, Joe*

Calling Time was first performed by the Bootleg Theatre Company in Salisbury on January 28th 2010 with the following cast:-

Kerry Stockwell
Sara Taylor
Stewart Taylor
Joe Bossano
Colin Burden

The play was directed by Colin Burden. Production Assistants were Adrian Cousins, Dean Ferguson and Sallie Lloyd. The scene entitled 'I know what you're thinking' has been added since this first production.

Intro
Cast *(in order of appearance)*

Bill   30s-40s, Publican, wearing open necked shirt and trousers

Tracy   20s - 30s, Bar Person (not seen)

The stage is set with typical pub tables and chairs. There are empty glasses on both tables. A man (Bill) enters. He picks up the glasses on one table and puts them down on the other. He sits down, and sighs. He looks at his watch then looks offstage and calls out.

Bill   Oh, for chrissake Tracy, I didn't mean nothing by it. Haven't you ever been touched by a man before? It is *not* sexual harassment. Sexual harassment is – well – sexual. Accidentally brushing my hand across your bum hardly qualifies. *(He looks at his watch again.)* Oh come on, get real will you? I hardly think it's fair leaving me to do all the clearing up – that's your job. It's what barmaids are supposed to do.

                  (We don't see Tracy, but just hear her.)

Tracy   *(off)* Bar person.

Bill   What?

Tracy   *(off)* Bar person. You shouldn't call me a barmaid.

Bill   *(to himself)* I know what I'd like to call you. *(Out loud)* All right bar person. Bar Person, will you please help me clear up ready?

Tracy   *(off)* When you apologise.

Bill   *(automatically)* I'm sorry.

Tracy   *(off)* As if you mean it.

Bill   *(sighs again.)* Tracy, I am truly sorry.

Tracy   *(off)* Don't patronise me.

Bill   I can't win can I?

Tracy   *(off)* No.

Bill   But can we get on now?

Tracy   *(off)* I suppose.

                  (Bill shakes his head with relief.)

Bill   *(to himself)* Thank God. *(Picks up all four glasses and goes off in the direction of Tracy.)*

Bill   Better watch out, here I come!

Blackout

Goodbye Simon
Cast *(in order of appearance)*

Janine *30s-40s, dressed in black*
Caroline
20s-30s, dressed in black

A woman, Janine, is sitting at one of the tables when Caroline appears coming towards her, carrying two vodka mixers.

Caroline There you go.

Janine Cheers. *(She takes a glass as Caroline sits down.)*

Caroline Well, it's over now.

Janine Yeah.

(They both take a drink.)

Caroline You OK, Janine?

Janine Yeah, I'll be fine.

Caroline Such a shame.

Janine Yeah. And so unexpected.

Caroline Hell of a shock.

Janine Shock, yeah you can say that again.

Caroline Still it was a nice ceremony – good turnout. And it was funny seeing Sue after all this time. I haven't seen her for years, have you?

Janine No. *(Pause.)* What did that bitch have to go and turn up for?

Caroline Sorry? Are you talking about the same Sue?

Janine Sue Slut – yes.

Caroline Why, what has she done?

Janine I thought you knew. I thought everyone knew. She and Simon were having it off.

Caroline What!

Janine It'd been going on for ages. They'd still be at it now if Simon hadn't have died.

Caroline Simon and Sue? You're joking!

Janine Wish I was. I knew you see. I *knew*. I could *smell* her on him.

Caroline Yes?

Janine He'd come home with a sort of smug look on his face. And he'd tell me a load of bollocks about where he's been. Work or something. I didn't believe a word of it. *(She takes another drink.)* Oh, I need this.

Caroline Do you forgive him now?

Janine	Forgive him? He's dead. What's to forgive? I certainly never forgave him when he was alive.
Caroline	I can't believe it.
Janine	Believe me Caroline, Simon was no saint.
	(A pause as Caroline takes a drink and hesitates.)
Caroline	No, I – I – er – know.
Janine	*(eyes Caroline suspiciously.)* Is there something you should be telling me?
Caroline	Some of the other people at the ceremony…
Janine	His friends you mean?
Caroline	I'm not sure they were all friends. *(She gulps some drink.)* I think some of them were there just to make sure…
Janine	Sure of what?
Caroline	That he was dead.
	(Janine can't believe what she hears. She stares at Caroline briefly, then laughs.)
Janine	What!
Caroline	I'm sorry I said anything.
Janine	You've said it now, so you can tell me what you mean.
Caroline	Well, he rather upset a lot of people. He didn't just lie to you, you know.
Janine	I guessed not.
Caroline	He was what you might call a con-artist too.
Janine	Yeah I know.
Caroline	And, well Janine the thing is, he was also a – a bit of a blackmailer...
Janine	I'm not surprised.
Caroline	You're not?
Janine	*(takes a drink.)* So, who was he blackmailing?
Caroline	Me among other people.
Janine	You? Now you do surprise me. What the hell for?
Caroline	*(sighing)* I suppose I can tell you now. It doesn't matter anymore. Anyway, it wasn't blackmailing, not really. Not in the ordinary sense. I mean he wasn't demanding money or anything. Just a few – favours – every now and then.
Janine	What sort of favours?
Caroline	He wanted me to sleep with him occasionally.
Janine	You! He slept with you too?
Caroline	Yes.
Janine	*(slams her glass back on the table.)* Jesus Christ! Was

	there nobody he wouldn't sleep with!
Caroline	Now hang on!
Janine	No, you hang on! I knew Simon put it about. I didn't expect my best friend to be on the receiving end!
Caroline	I had no choice. I told you, he made me. He threatened to tell John otherwise.
Janine	Tell John what? What did Simon threaten to tell John?
Caroline	That I was two-timing him.
Janine	And were you?
	(Pause.)
Caroline	Yes.
Janine	So who else were you seeing?
Caroline	Tony
Janine	Tony? Do I know Tony?
Caroline	My boss.
Janine	*(picks up her drink and takes a gulp.)* Now let me get this straight. You slept with my husband because he threatened to tell your boyfriend that you were sleeping with your boss?
Caroline	Silly isn't it?
Janine	Silly? Well, yes that's one way of putting it.
Caroline	I don't know what else to say.
Janine	Well it's over now. In a way you must be relieved.
Caroline	Oh, that's an awful thing to say! I wouldn't have wished him dead!
Janine	Wouldn't you?
Caroline	No… of course not. I mean who would ever have imagined the electric blanket would be live like that?
Janine	Must have shorted somehow.
Caroline	Even so, had he not had a dicky heart he might still be here.
Janine	That's true.
Caroline	Still it looks like you're coping alright on your own.
Janine	Yes, no problem. I've been keeping myself good and busy.
Caroline	Best thing.
Janine	Yeah, I've been doing evening classes. Funny thing, I started one only a couple of weeks before Simon's accident.
Caroline	Really, doing what?

Janine	DIY. Basic stuff mainly. Mending a fuse… Wiring plugs… Electric circuits, that sort of thing... Still you never know when it might come in handy. *(She looks at her watch.)* Oh is that the time? I must fly. *(Janine gets up.)* Thanks for the drink, Caroline. Bye, see you later! *(She exits, leaving Caroline staring after her dumfounded as the truth dawns.)*

Blackout

What's Yours?
Cast *(in order of appearance)*

Paul – 20s-30s in casual jacket and trousers – mobile phone in pocket
Emma – 20s-40s, smart casual clothes with shoulder bag, inside is a purse and credit card wallet
A man (Paul) is sitting with a drink – a half pint which is only half full – at one of the tables. He looks around, then fixes his attention on his drink. A few moments later a woman (Emma) comes in with a drink. She has a shoulder bag which she puts down as she sits at another table and takes a sip at her drink, occasionally glancing up at Paul. He starts to say something, but stops himself. She too looks like she wants to say something. When, eventually, they both speak they do so at the same time.

Emma	Are y–
Paul	Are you..?
Emma	Paul?
Paul	Emma?
	(They both laugh.)
Paul	Can I? *(He gets up and goes towards Emma's table.)*
Emma	Of course.
Paul	*(goes over to her table and sits.)* Sorry, I wasn't sure to start with... you're not –
Emma	Not what? Not what you expected?
Paul	Well ah –
Emma	I'm older than you thought I'd be, is that it?
Paul	Not exactly...
Emma	You were expecting a size 10, I suppose?
Paul	No – I...
Emma	Taller then?

Paul	No – oh look, forget it.
Emma	What then?
Paul	Well, you're not exactly how you described yourself in your email, are you?
Emma	You're disappointed. *(Pause.)* So I used a little creative licence. Looks aren't everything you know.
Paul	I know. And it doesn't matter... really.
Emma	Not getting off to a very good start are we?
Paul	No... sorry.
Emma	Let's start again, shall we?
Paul	Good idea. Hi, Emma? I'm Paul. *(Smiles and holds out his hand.)*
Emma	Hi, good to see you.
Paul	Good to see you.
Emma	Were you waiting long?
Paul	No, no time at all really.
Emma	Good.
	(There's an awkward silence.)
Paul	You've got a drink?
Emma	*(Smiling)* Yes. Yes thanks. *(She sips it.)*
Paul	Good. I've never done this before you know. *(He sips his drink.)*
Emma	Been to a pub? Talked to a woman?
Paul	*(Laughing)* No, you know, met someone through the internet. Never done it before.
Emma	Haven't you?
Paul	No. Have you?
Emma	Once.
Paul	Right. *(He takes another sip of his drink.)* What do you do?
Emma	As in work?
Paul	Yes.
Emma	Nothing at the moment. I'm planning to start looking for a job next week.
Paul	Oh, what sort of thing?
Emma	Anything really. Whatever. Office, shop, doesn't matter. Just something to pay the bills, you know. And you?
Paul	Same. There's not a lot on the market though.
Emma	No. Do you live round here then?

(He takes another sip and so does she.)

Paul	A bit out of town, just off the London Road.
Emma	Really? Me too!
Paul	No! Whereabouts?
Emma	Do you know Crowthorne Street?
Paul	I live in Crowthorne Street!
Emma	Never!
Paul	Number 14. I'm renting a studio flat.
Emma	I'm just up the road – Number 5!
Paul	That is really spooky.
Emma	You're telling me. So how long have you been there?
Paul	Oh, only a month or so.
Emma	Just a bit longer than me then!
Paul	So where were you before?
Emma	Oh – ah – London.
Paul	Bit quieter here then?
Emma	Certainly is. That was the attraction I think. I mean London's great if you've got money and that. But – well, it's just a rat race otherwise isn't it?
Paul	I suppose so. Depends what you're doing. *(He takes another sip – the glass should be nearly empty by now.)*
Emma	Yeah. Well I couldn't stand it. Had to get out. *(Pause.)* And you?
Paul	Oh, well I came from around here originally. Went to college here. But I've been away.
Emma	Anywhere nice?
Paul	No, not really. Not nice at all really.
Emma	Oh so why'd you go. Did work take you or something?
Paul	Something like that. You could call it work, yes.
Emma	So what do you do? You said you were looking for a job. What is it you do?
Paul	Oh, this and that.
Emma	You're being very mysterious.
Paul	It wasn't much of a job.
Emma	*(laughs.)* Oh, come on! It can't be that bad.
Paul	Honestly. *(He takes a drink and finds he's finished it.)*
Emma	Can I get you another?
Paul	No, no I should get you one.

Emma   I haven't finished this one yet! Come on, I'll get you one.
            What's your poison?
Paul   That's nice of you. Ah, well, half of 6X I think it was.
Emma   Fine.
            *(She dives into her shoulder bag and extracts a purse,
            picks up his empty glass and exits. Paul sits there for a
            second or two looking around. His eye catches the bag
            and he glances around again before reaching over and
            opening the bag. He reaches in and extracts a wallet
            containing credit cards which he flicks through quickly. He
            looks at them undecided, then with emphasis he replaces
            them in the bag. He sits for a few seconds, taking deep
            breaths, then pulls a mobile phone from his pocket and
            keys in a number.)*
Paul   Hi, it's Paul – Paul Edwards. You said to ring if, if ever I
            needed to. If ever I was – tempted *(Pause.)* No, no it's all
            right, I haven't done anything, don't worry. But you said to
            ring anyway. It was important you said – *(Pause.)* What?
            (Pause.) No, exactly. Yes, yes, I feel quite pleased with
            myself. I resisted you see. *(Beat.)* Yes, really. *(Pause.)* It
            was a load of credit cards. I had them in my hands. I
            would have taken them I know I would. Before, I wouldn't
            have given it a second thought. *(Pause.)* Yes, I know. I do
            yes. I actually feel proud of myself. It's a weird feeling you
            know. Really strange. Look I'd better not talk too long,
            she'll come back in a minute. *(Pause.)* Gone to get me a
            drink. *(He laughs.)* Yes, I know. And you don't mind me
            calling like this? *(Pause.)* No, no I know. Funny this you
            know, feeling good about myself for once. *(Pause.)* Yes,
            you too. Yeah, cheers Dan I appreciate it. *(He pushes a
            button on the phone and replaces it in his pocket, then sits
            back in his chair and looks around just as Emma
            reappears with a pint of beer which she puts on the table
            in front of him and tosses her purse back in her bag.)*
Emma   There you go!
Paul   A pint – thanks! I thought you were just getting me a half.
Emma   Do you good.
Paul   Well, cheers! *(He picks up the pint and takes a good swig.
            Emma picks up her glass and joins him.)*
Emma   Cheers!
Paul   Mm that's nice.
Emma   Who was on the phone then?

Paul	Phone?
Emma	You were on your mobile just now.
Paul	Was I?
Emma	Yes. I saw you as I came back in.
Paul	Oh no one. A friend that's all.
Emma	I see. *(Pause.)* How long have you've been living here? A month or so, wasn't it?
Paul	Yeah.
Emma	And where were you before did you say?
Paul	I didn't.
Emma	You've been inside haven't you?
Paul	Inside? Inside where?
Emma	*(laughing)* Come on, you don't fool me! I can tell. You have, haven't you? Done time?
Paul	What – what makes you say that? *(He nervously picks up his pint and takes a gulp.)*
Emma	I can tell. I can see the signs. I recognise them. It takes one to know one you know!
Paul	Sorry?
Emma	Come on, what were you in for?
Paul	Petty larceny.
	(Emma immediately dives into her bag and extracts the credit card case, which she checks.)
Paul	It's all right, I didn't touch it.
Emma	You mean you didn't take it?
Paul	Correct.
Emma	So you're going straight?
Paul	Trying to.
Emma	I'm impressed.
Paul	It's not easy. *(He takes another sip.)*
Emma	I'm sure no one told you it was.
Paul	So you don't mind?
Emma	Mind? No, why should I?
Paul	You know, drinking with an ex-con.
Emma	But you're an *ex*-con – that's the main thing.
Paul	Trying to be.
Emma	Well, good for you. You're making an effort to reform yourself. That's good.
Paul	Yeah.

Emma	Wish I could.
Paul	Wish you could what?
Emma	Reform myself. Must be nice, that.
Paul	Are you saying -
Emma	Course! Couldn't you tell?
Paul	So you moved here from where exactly?
Emma	Holloway.
Paul	As in Islington?
Emma	As in prison.
Paul	Ah, right... So, er, what were you doing there?
Emma	Five years.
Paul	*(takes another sip as he absorbs this information.)* And what were you doing five years for?
Emma	Manslaughter.
Paul	Manslaughter! *(He gulps down some beer.)*
Emma	Yeah, they couldn't make a murder charge stick you see. *(Paul is becoming visibly agitated by now.)*
Paul	I see. *(Pause.)* Are you saying it – it *was* murder?
Emma	Of course. Still it's all water under the bridge now isn't it?
Paul	And – who... who did you – you know...?
Emma	Oh it wasn't just one. There were three of them, just men I met up with, that's all. But they only got me for the one. He was a sweety really. I mean I liked him. But, ah well c'est la vie.
Paul	And how did you... um...
Emma	Poison. I poisoned them. I just can't help myself you see, that's the trouble.

Blackout

Mr Critchley, Isn't It?
Cast *(in order of appearance)*

Kathy – *20s - 30s, smartly dressed newspaper reporter with shoulder bag containing digital recorder, a notebook and photograph*

Adrian – *30s - 50s. smartly dressed MP*

The tables are empty as the lights come up. A woman (Kathy) enters followed by a man (Adrian). they both have drinks in their hands. She also has a shoulder bag. She goes over to one of the empty tables.

Kathy   We'll sit here shall we?

Adrian   If you like. That's fine.

    (They both sit and she puts the shoulder bag beside her on the floor.)

Kathy   I wonder, do you mind? *(Reaches into her bag and brings out a voice recorder.)*

Adrian   What? Oh no, go ahead.

Kathy   I find it so much easier to record it than make notes. And my shorthand is useless. Well, worse than useless really.

Adrian   I thought all reporters did shorthand as a matter of course.

Kathy   Not any longer. Besides this is so much more accurate. No chance of me misquoting you with this is there?

Adrian   I should hope not. I've had enough misquotes to last me a lifetime.

Kathy   A parliamentary lifetime?

Adrian   If you like?

Kathy   Right, well where would you like to start?

Adrian   You're the one who asked for the interview. I assumed you would know where you wanted to start. And let's not rake up all that stuff about expenses, eh? It's all old hat by now.

Kathy   I thought I could start by – Oh, it would help if I switched this on wouldn't it? *(She switches on the recorder and leans towards it.)* Kathy James interview with Adrian Critchley. Right, Adrian – you don't mind if I call you Adrian do you?

Adrian   Of course not, it's my name.

Kathy   Good. Well, let's start – Adrian – by talking about the SouthMead shopping centre proposal. What have you got against it?

Adrian   I thought my views were well known already. But I'm happy to reiterate them. I'm always glad of an opportunity to make the case for the honest decent traders in this

	town – people who are going to see their trade decimated if SouthMead gets planning approval.

Kathy   Isn't that a bit melodramatic?

Adrian   Not at all. It'll take trade out of the town, sure as eggs are eggs.

Kathy   Presumably because the price of eggs will be a lot less in SouthMead?

Adrian   That is hardly the point.

Kathy   What exactly is the point then, Mr Critchley?

Adrian   The consumer will lose out in the end. Oh yes, they may be able to buy a few groceries for a bit less.

Kathy   A lot less, wouldn't you say?

Adrian   I would not. But saving a few quid here and then will do nothing to compensate them for what they will lose?

Kathy   No?

Adrian   No. Shops here in the town centre will shut. This pub could well end up closing too if custom drops off any further. Pubs are closing at an alarming rate anyway. So the result will be a ghost town with none of the diversity and interesting shops we have now. Just the big national chains, selling the same homogeneous crap – sorry, I mean an identical product offering – as you get in every other shopping centre the length and breadth of this land.

Kathy   But that isn't the real reason you're so against the shopping centre proposal is it – Adrian?

Adrian   Sorry? *(He takes a swig of his drink.)*

Kathy   Doesn't your antipathy to the scheme have rather more to do with your mistress?

Adrian   *(splutters drink over the table.)* What did you say?

Kathy   Oh, I think you heard me perfectly clearly.

Adrian   This interview is at an end.

Kathy   Oh why? We've only just started.

Adrian   I have nothing more to say.

Kathy   Oh of course you do. You do yourself down, Adrian. I'm sure you have plenty to say.

Adrian   Not to you.

Kathy   I'll just go ahead and print what I've got then shall I?

Adrian   You haven't got anything.

Kathy   Oh believe me I have, Adrian.

Adrian   Mr Critchley.

Kathy	Mr Critchley.
Adrian	You print libellous stuff like that and I'll sue you so fast your feet won't touch the floor.
Kathy	I'm not sure I understood that.
Adrian	You know what I mean.
Kathy	Oh I know what you mean, Adri— Mr Critchley. But it's only libellous if it's not true, isn't that right? I mean you have got a mistress haven't you?
Adrian	No, I have not.
Kathy	Such a quaintly old-fashioned word isn't it? Mistress...
Adrian	I told you I do not have a – I have nothing of the kind. You just scent blood don't you? You're all the same, you bloody journalists. Just because we've had a bit of an image problem lately, you think you can go in for the kill on any pretext. Well you've met your match with me, I can tell you that. In all the furore there was, nobody came up with any scandal about me. You don't catch me sticking my fingers in the till.
Kathy	No one caught you, no. But I wasn't thinking about a till you were sticking your fingers in...
Adrian	How dare you?
Kathy	Oh very easily believe me.
Adrian	You have nothing on me. Nothing at all.
Kathy	No? Well, perhaps you should take a look... *(She reaches into her bag and extracts a photograph.)* at this.
Adrian	What have you got there?
Kathy	It looks to me like a photograph... of one Adrian Critchley MP, in what can only be described as a passionate embrace with one Miss Linda Bellingham. Miss Bellingham is a particularly close associate of yours is she, Adrian?
Adrian	Give me that!
Kathy	Not so fast.
Adrian	I said give me that bloody photograph! *(He stands up suddenly, knocking the chair over, and tries to grab the photograph from her hands.)*
Kathy	Uh, uh. Mine I think.
Adrian	Give me the bloody thing! *(He grabs her hand and begins to wrestle the photograph from her.)*
Kathy	Ow! You're hurting me... People are looking. You don't want to attract too much attention do you?

Adrian   Let them look. *(Finally he prises the photograph from her and proceeds to tear it up in little pieces.)*

Kathy   It's digital. And there are plenty more on my computer.

Adrian   We'll have the police round to see about them!

Kathy   Now you don't really want the police round looking at all the photographs I have of you and Miss Bellingham, do you?

Adrian   *(returns to his seat and sits.)* What do you want?

Kathy   It's interesting isn't it, that Linda Bellingham is a partner in Cooper Associates who just happen to own a useful parcel of land in the high street that includes the old primary school. In a thriving community, that could be a prime retail site. But not if SouthMead goes ahead and retailers here start going bust. Not good for business that.

Adrian   Are you suggesting I'm colluding with this Cooper Associates, using my influence as an MP to try and stop SouthMead. Is that what you're saying?

Kathy   I couldn't have put it better myself.

Adrian   *(suddenly realises that the recorder is still running.)* Switch that bloody thing off!

Kathy   Sorry?

Adrian   You heard me.

Kathy   I thought you said you had no objections to our interview being taped?

Adrian   I have plenty of objections to a little tart like you trying to set me up!

Kathy   Set you up? Surely not. I was merely pointing out that your – association – with Linda Bellingham might not leave you in a particularly good light with your constituents. Not to mention your wife.

Adrian   You're a right little bitch aren't you?

Kathy   Oh, I do hope not.

Adrian   Now will you switch that think off or do I have to throw it out the window?

Kathy   That would be a waste. They're quite expensive these little things you know. But amazing quality. *(She picks it up and holds it out to him.)* Would you like to listen?

Adrian   No I would not..

Kathy   Pity. *(She switches the recorder off.)* There, is that better? *(Pause.)*

Adrian   So what are you after?

Kathy   What is any newspaper after, Mr Critchley, the truth of course.

Adrian   Hah! The truth? Your sort don't know the meaning of the word.

Kathy   Oh I think our sort do. For example... *(Again she reaches into her bag, this time extracting a notebook.)* Let me see. *(She flicks through several pages.)* On the 22nd April, you and Linda were seen entering the Holiday Inn in Southampton at 7.30pm where you stayed until 8.15 the following morning.

Adrian   Is that it?

Kathy   No, it gets worse. The following Thursday you stayed in a Travelodge.

Adrian   I can do without the jokes.

Kathy   I'm sure you can. But let's face it Adrian, you're a bit of a joke aren't you? What's up, wouldn't your expenses run to anything a bit more upmarket? Hardly calculated to impress our Linda is it? I'm sure she's used to much better.

Adrian   Will you shut the fuck up!

Kathy   Sorry, not upsetting you am I?

Adrian   *(takes a deep breath.)* Even if this were all true. Which it isn't. It's hardly front page news is it? I've done nothing illegal.

Kathy   No that's right, cheating on your wife isn't illegal. Quite correct. And shagging the partner in a land investment company doesn't constitute fraud. And you're quite entitled to campaign against the shopping centre development. No problem with that. But you do see, don't you Adrian – I mean you're a bright guy and all that – you do see that it won't look particularly well with your voters will it? All those loyal people who have supported you through thick and thin. I mean, if MPs were rated a bit higher than estate agents and, dare I say journalists, there might be some hope, But, let's face it, you are at the bottom of the heap, aren't you? So really anything you can do to preserve your name would be of benefit wouldn't you say?

Adrian   What, for the last time, do you want?

Kathy   Five grand.

Adrian   What?

Kathy   You do have trouble with your hearing don't you?

Adrian   Go screw yourself.

Kathy	Is that your best offer?
Adrian	You print any of this and I'll see that you are well and truly screwed, see if I don't!
Kathy	Not by you I hope. I know you have a tendency to put it about a bit, but that really is above and beyond... *(Once again Adrian jumps out of his chair and goes for her, but stops himself and returns to his seat.)*
Adrian	You think you've got me don't you?
Kathy	By the balls.
Adrian	Well I'm sorry to disappoint you.
Kathy	You're saying there's nothing between you and Linda are you? You're saying *(She flicks through her notebook.)* that all these *very* detailed accounts and photographic evidence of your affair with her are pure fantasy. Is that what you're saying?
Adrian	I'm saying I'm not going to be blackmailed by a little shit like you for five grand! Five grand – you have got to be joking! You just plucked that figure out of the air I suppose. You've been watching too many movies. I'm not paying you five thousand pounds for a few photographs and a scruffy notebook. What do you take me for?
Kathy	A cheating cheapskate of an MP.
Adrian	Whatever you're accusing me of, I haven't done anything illegal. Whereas, blackmail is a serious crime.
Kathy	I'd look on it more as insurance.
Adrian	Would you? Would you indeed? I think the police would be very interested in your little game.
Kathy	I think the public would be very interested in yours.
Adrian	Publish and be damned as Oscar Wilde said.
Kathy	I think you'll find it was the Duke of Wellington.
Adrian	I don't give a fuck who it was.
Kathy	Why doesn't that surprise me? You don't really give a toss for anyone do you? All you think about is yourself. The great Adrian Critchley.
Adrian	I'm not paying you a penny.
Kathy	No? I think you will. Just think for a moment about all you'll be losing. A few thousand is small beer compared with that.
Adrian	I'm calling your bluff.
Kathy	It's no bluff, believe me. If you don't want to see your photograph splashed across the front pages, I suggest

	you listen to me.
Adrian	Listen to you? A jumped up little blackmailing hack from the local rag?
Kathy	If you value your career you will.
Adrian	Oh really?
	(Pause.)
Kathy	Well, what is it to be: yes or no?
	(Adrian gets up and stands on his chair.)
Kathy	What are you doing?
	(He ignores her and addresses everyone in the pub, i.e. the audience.)
Adrian	Ladies and gentlemen, could I have your attention please? My name is Adrian Critchley. I'm an MP. But, perhaps, not for much longer. I am, I have to tell you, having an affair. Now you might not be surprised at that. You might think that it's what all MPs get up to at one time or another. Actually you would be wrong. But that's not the point. I am not proud of what I have done. Equally I am not sorry. My marriage is on the rocks. It has been for the past three years. I know it. My wife knows it. It seems the only person who doesn't know it is the woman sitting here. Her name is Kathy. she is a journalist and she has documentary evidence of my infidelity. Furthermore, she has just announced that she will publish full details of my affair together with photographic evidence in her newspaper unless I pay her five thousand pounds. That I believe is a criminal act which I cannot and will not be cowed by. I will not be blackmailed. Among you I'm sure are people who have voted for me in the past. Having now heard what I have done, if you decided not to vote for me in the future, I wouldn't be surprised. But just consider this: I no longer love my wife and she no longer loves me. I do however love the woman I am accused of having an affair with. That is my crime. Thank you. *(He gets down off the table.)*
Kathy	*(sighing)* Very clever. *(Pause.)* I'll take that as a 'no' then, shall I?

Blackout

I Know What You're Thinking
Cast *(in order of appearance)*
Tim - 20s-30s
Rebecca - 20s-30s

Rebecca comes in. She looks around. She has a drink in her hand. Tim is sitting at a table on his own, also with a drink. She approaches him and indicates the seat.

Rebecca	This free?
Tim	Think so. Help yourself.

(She sits down, purposely turning the chair so she is not facing him. He takes a drink, eyeing her. She looks at her watch. She takes a drink. She taps the table. She takes another sip of drink. He looks again at her more quizzically. She pointedly ignores him. He takes another sip of his drink, before asking)

Tim	Excuse me for asking, but is anything wrong?
Rebecca	Wrong?
Tim	You seem a little... perturbed?
Rebecca	Perturbed?
Tim	Agitated maybe.
Rebecca	I am not agitated thank you very much.
Tim	If you say so.
Rebecca	I say so.

(Pause.)

Tim	I'd say you weren't normally like this.
Rebecca	Excuse me, who are you to say what I'm normally like?
Tim	I'd say you were usually – well – pretty laid back.
Rebecca	I don't know how you could possibly know that.
Tim	But it's true?
Rebecca	I don't actually see that's any of your business.
Tim	No, guess not.

(Pause during which they eye each other. He takes a drink and smiles.)

Tim	I know what you're thinking. You're thinking: 'Have I met this bloke before?'
Rebecca	*(shakes her head in disbelief.)* Well that's where you're wrong. I was actually thinking 'Who is this Muppet?'
Tim	*(laughs.)* No you're not.
Rebecca	Sorry?
Tim	You're not thinking that at all.

Rebecca	Who are you to tell me what I'm thinking? I know what I'm thinking.
Tim	I beg to differ.
Rebecca	Yeah, well that's as maybe. *(She gets up.)* Excuse me.
Tim	Are you going somewhere?
Rebecca	Anywhere you're not. If it's all the same to you. *(Starts off.)*
Tim	He won't be there.
	(She looks back with a withering look before continuing.)
Tim	Giles. He won't be there. You're wasting your time.
	(She stops, questioning, then comes back.)
Rebecca	You know Giles?
Tim	I know of him. Never had the pleasure of actually meeting him.
Rebecca	I don't understand. *(She sits.)*
Tim	You were planning to meet him in the other bar, but he never showed. You're thinking you'll have another look, but you know he won't be there. Don't you?
Rebecca	What kind of trick is this?
Tim	No trick.
Rebecca	I don't get it.
Tim	I told you: I know what you're thinking.
Rebecca	Oh yeah?
Tim	Right now you're thinking: 'Maybe I should play along with him for a bit. He interests me.'
Rebecca	*(laughs.)* Hah! I'll tell you what I'm thinking: 'why am I listening to this over-inflated ego prattle on?' – that's what I'm thinking. You're unbelievable.
Tim	But you are intrigued.
Rebecca	*(picks up her drink and stands up to go.)* Goodbye.
Tim	Thinking of going round Amanda's are you?
Rebecca	None of your business.
Tim	I mean you can't go back to yours now can you? Kind of burnt your bridges there haven't you?
Rebecca	Do I know you? *(Puts her drink back down.)*
Tim	Do you want to?
Rebecca	Very definitely not.
Tim	But...?
Rebecca	But nothing.
Tim	So what are you going to do now? I mean it's over between you and Justin, you know that. You never really

thought it would work out anyway, did you? And Giles has obviously decided to do a runner. So that relationship is going nowhere either is it?

Rebecca You don't know that.

Tim I don't know that, no. I'm merely reporting back what you thoughts are on the matter. As I said, I don't even know the bloke.

Rebecca What do you want?

Tim I don't want anything.

Rebecca No? Good. *(She picks up her drink and downs the remains.)*

Rebecca But, before you ask, I do.

Tim You do... what?

Rebecca I would like another drink, thank you. *(She sits.)*

Tim Oh, right...

Rebecca You were thinking of asking me, weren't you?
(He doesn't answer.)

Rebecca Oh, come on, don't deny it.

Tim I – well, since you're here... and your glass is empty... I suppose... What were you drinking exactly?

Rebecca I think you know that don't you?

Tim *(smiles.)* Don't really have to ask do I?

Rebecca No.
(He picks up her glass to get a refill.)

Rebecca My God.

Tim What?

Rebecca Italian. I adore Italian.

Tim Am I missing something?

Rebecca You were wondering what food I like.
(Pause.)

Tim Maybe.

Rebecca Yes, you were... My God, that's amazing. It is you, isn't it? It is you that I'm hearing?

Tim How would I know?

Rebecca It's a weird experience isn't it? Like overhearing someone at a noisy party. You know, like when you can pick out what someone's saying on the other side of the room? You kind of block out all the other noise. Is it like that for you?

Tim Sort of... So what about now?

Rebecca	What about now, what? Oh, I see... Well... a seafood risotto I think. And you're wondering if I'm vegetarian? I'm not as it happens.
Tim	Good. *(He puts the glass back down.)* I know a very nice little Italian in Grosvenor Street: Caravaggio's. Or what about Piccolo Diavolo?
Rebecca	Little Devil.
Tim	Me?
Rebecca	The name of the restaurant: Piccolo Diavolo.
Tim	Oh I see. Well, I like Little Devil better than a Muppet with a – what was it? – an over-inflated ego.
Rebecca	That was before I knew what you were really thinking.
Tim	So... does a meal appeal?
Rebecca	Yes and–
Tim	And?
Rebecca	And... no, you're trying to block me, aren't you? You're trying to think of something else!
Tim	I've no idea what you mean.
Rebecca	*(laughs.)* Oh, yeah!
Tim	So Caravaggio's. Or Piccolo Diavolo?
Rebecca	I'll leave it up to you.
Tim	Is that wise?
Rebecca	Remember I know what you're thinking.
Tim	Ah, right... So what am I thinking right now?
Rebecca	You're... thinking... *(She smiles.)* Really?
Tim	Really.
Rebecca	Well, I'm not sure...
Tim	No?
Rebecca	Well see. *(She recognises another one of his thoughts and looks shocked. He realises she's read his thoughts.)*
Tim	Oh, I'm sorry I wasn't thinking.
Rebecca	You were – and that's the trouble.
Tim	I know what it must seem like. But I didn't mean it like that!
Rebecca	I'll let you off. *(Pause.)* Well, shall we go?
Tim	*(stands up and indicates for her to go first.)* After you.
Rebecca	*(gets up and starts off. She stops and turns to him.)* And if you imagine you're going to do that, you've got another think coming...
Tim	Sorry.

Rebecca	Yeah, well mind what you're thinking. *(She searches his face, recognises something and smiles.)*
Rebecca	So – what then?
Tim	*(laughs.)* I'm thinking about it.

Blackout

Who's Joe?
Cast *(in order of appearance)*

Simon
30s-40s, typical businessman type, in suit
Joe
20s-30s in jeans and trainers carrying sports bag

At one of the tables, Simon is sitting reading a newspaper, a pint of beer in front of him when Joe arrives. He has a sports bag in his hand which he puts down alongside the vacant chair opposite Simon. Joe has a pronounced Eastern European accent.

Joe	I sit here?
Simon	*(lowers his newspaper slightly.)* It's free if that's what you mean.
Joe	I am sitting here?
Simon	If you want.
Joe	*(sits)* You drink beer?
Simon	It's a pub. That's what you do. *(Pause.)* Aren't you drinking?
Joe	I have no money.
Simon	Ah, I see.
Joe	I have no money.
Simon	I heard you.
Joe	You have money?
Simon	I have plenty of money, thank you very much. But I'm afraid I intend holding on to it. So, if you're after a hand-out, I have to say, sorry you're out of luck.
Joe	I not want your money! What I want with your money?
Simon	To buy a drink I suppose.
Joe	I not want your money!
Simon	Good.
	(Simon pointedly picks up his newspaper and begins

reading. Joe reaches over and pulls down a corner of the paper to look at Simon.)

Simon Excuse me!

Joe You have car?

Simon Car? Yes, I've got a car. Why?

Joe Bad, very bad. All place bad news tomorrow.

Simon Sorry? What are you talking about?

Joe I tell you is bad tomorrow. For all peoples. You have car, you leave.

Simon I'm having a drink. That's why I'm in a pub. Then, after I've finished, I'm going home.

Joe I need car. Need to go long way.

Simon Well, you're not having mine. Where are you planning on going?

Joe Away. Away from fascist police. They hunt me. Always, they hunt me.

Simon Look, I really don't follow you...

Joe No not you. Filthy police. They follow me.

Simon And why would the police be after you?

Joe They want me. Want torture. Beat me.

Simon I don't think so.

Joe What you know? You sit here with drink. What you worry about my peoples?

Simon What *are you* going on about?

Joe Oh, yes, it all right for you. Yes? You don't care what happens in my country. You only care what happens here.

Simon Sorry?

Joe You not hear what I say?

Simon Yes I heard you. But, if you don't mind, I'd like to get on with my paper.

Joe *(stands up angrily.)* You think I stupid. Is that it? You think I stupid?

Simon No – no – I. Look, sit down will you?

Joe Why I sit down?

Simon *(patronisingly)* Because if people are after you as you say, you'll be attracting attention to yourself won't you?

Joe So you not care what happens here?

Simon Oh, look why don't you go and bother someone else? Look I'll tell you what, why don't you go and sit over there?

Joe Because I talk to you.

Simon	Well I'm not sure I want to talk to you, if that's all right. I'd just like to be left in peace with my pint and my newspaper.
Joe	You want left in peace? You want left in peace! I not leave you in peace!
Simon	You've made that very plain. Look, I don't know who you are and I have to say, I don't really care, but whoever you are, will you please — piss off!
Joe	You want me piss off?
Simon	That would be very helpful. Yes, please, I'd appreciate that.
Joe	I am looking you.
Simon	Looking me?
Joe	*(pulls out a plastic identity card from his pocket and thrusts it at Simon.)* I am looking you my card. This say who I am.
Simon	What?
Joe	This tell you.
Simon	Yes, yes, so you're Slovakian. I see. So what?
Joe	No! There you have it wrong Mr Smart Ass! You think you smart yes? Well you not.
Simon	What the hell are you talking about? Look, I'd really rather get on with my paper and pint in peace, if it's all the same to you.
Joe	I not Slovak.
Simon	That's not what your identity card says.
Joe	I steal card.
Simon	I see.
Joe	What you see? You see nothing!
Simon	I see a rude foreign bastard who is starting to annoy me a great deal. And I'm warning you —
Joe	You no warn me. I warn you!
Simon	Oh, for Christ's sake... what do you want exactly?
Joe	You not listen.
Simon	I heard you. It just didn't make much sense that's all.
Joe	Then you want listen good, mister.
Simon	On the contrary, I think you want listen good. Let me say it again, so you haven't got any excuse. I'll speak nice and slowly, all right? Ready? Just - go - away - will - you?
Joe	You make big mistake.

Simon	No, my friend, you make big mistake. You made a big mistake by walking in here.
Joe	Why you call me friend?
Simon	It's a turn of phrase. It doesn't mean anything.
Joe	You want be my friend?
Simon	No, I don't. I certainly do not want to be your friend! Frankly it's the last thing I want.
Joe	You not like me?
Simon	*(laughs.)* You have to ask? Jesus.,.
Joe	What your problem?
Simon	My problem! I haven't got a problem. Except you!
Joe	You think I am problem? I tell you what problem is. Ja, I tell you problem all right. You in big problem. You! Outside this place, in street outside, they in problem too.
Simon	Who?
Joe	People here. People out in street No one safe. Not now. Maybe if you listen, maybe you do something. But you not. You not do anything. You not think. *(He stands up and gesticulates at his temple, standing over Simon.)* You not think! You make mistake. Big mistake.
Simon	What the hell are you talking about? You are beginning to bore me you know. You are really beginning to bore me. And, since it seems that you are not prepared to piss off quietly as you were asked, I suppose it only leaves it for me to do so. *(Simon folds his paper, finishes most of his pint, and stands up.)*
Joe	Where you go?
Simon	Out. Away. Anywhere frankly, where you are not.
Joe	You not leave.
Simon	Well you're wrong there, mate, because I'm off. Cheerio, it's been — an experience — meeting you.
Joe	I tell you, you not leave.
Simon	Wrong.
Joe	*(grabs Simon's arm.)* You not leave!
Simon	Let go of my arm. *(Pause.)* Will you let go of my arm please?
Joe	You stay. I need tell you.
Simon	*(shakes his arm free.)* Tell me what? I'm not interested, whatever it is.
Joe	I warn you bad day. Big mess.

Simon	Mess? What sort of mess?
Joe	Many die.
Simon	Die? Who's going to die?
Joe	All peoples who are against us. All who not support our struggle.
Simon	Are you talking about some sort of terrorist threat?
Joe	Terrorist yes. Bad men. Here. Now. Fascist police. They not stop us.
Simon	What are you saying?
Joe	What your name?
Simon	Hardly any of your business. But it's Simon.
Joe	Joe. My name Joe. I like you Simon. I no want hurt you.
Simon	I'm pleased to hear it.
Joe	That's why you take car now and go far away.
Simon	No, no... I don't know what you are on about.... But, frankly I think this whole charade has gone far enough. *(There's a long pause, then Joe lightens and smiles.)*
Joe	You're right. I'm sorry.
Simon	Sorry?
	(Another pause. Joe's voice has suddenly become perfectly ordinary English.)
Joe	I can't keep this up! *(He laughs.)* Sorry.
Simon	*(stares at him in disbelief.)* You're not Slovak?
Joe	No. Born in Bury actually. Brought up in Brighton.
Simon	*(at a loss for words.)* So what was that all about?
Joe	Just wanted to see your reaction, you know. *(Pause.)*
Simon	My reaction should have been to call the police. Not just tell you to piss off.
Joe	But you didn't.
Simon	No. You're very lucky I didn't. *(He shakes his head.)* Jesus! That was not amusing. Not in the slightest bit funny.
Joe	Sorry.
Simon	What was that for? A bet or something?
Joe	Something like that. Not everything is what it seems you see.
Simon	So I see.
Joe	I'd better get going.

Simon	Right. Yes, I think you'd better.
Joe	Got a lot to do today.
Simon	No doubt.
Joe	Enjoy your paper.
Simon	Yes.

(Joe goes off and Simon watches him, sipping his drink. He picks up his paper and unfolds it to read. As he does so, Simon sees the bag that Joe brought in with him, still by the chair He picks it up and holds it out.)

Simon Here you've forgotten your bag! Where's he gone? *(Turning to others in pub.)* Did you see where that bloke went? He's left his bag here. *(He slowly turns to look at bag with increasing suspicion.)*

Blackout

Outro
Cast *(in order of appearance)*
Tracy
20s-30s, bar person, jeans T-shirt
Bill
30s-40s, (not seen)

The glass that Simon was drinking from is still on one table. Tracy enters, yelling backwards into the wings.

Tracy Do that again and I'll – I'll swing for you!
(She picks up the glass and as she does do, she notices something on the floor. She replaces the glass and bends down. When she stands up she has a number of pieces of the photograph, which Adrian tore up, in her hand. She spreads them out on the table like a jigsaw puzzle.)

Tracy What's this? Oh, I see. Mm, well that rather interesting. Is that what I think it is? And what's his hand doing there? He's worse than Bill.
(She collects the pieces of photograph up and deposits them in the glass.)
(We hear, but don't see, Bill.)

Bill *(off)* Give us a hand here will you Tracy?
(Tracy tuts to herself, sighs and exits. As she disappears from sight, we hear her trip over something and the sound of a glass smashing.)

Tracy *(off)* Shit! Who left that bloody bag there?
Curtain

Properties List
Intro
On tables:　　　　　　Four empty glasses

Goodbye Simon
Off stage:　　　　　　Two vodka mixers

What's yours?
On table:　　　　　　Half pint
Paul (personal):　　Mobile phone
Off Stage:
Emma (personal):　Bag containing credit card wallet

Mr Critchley, Isn't It?
Off Stage

　　　　　　　　　　Two drinks. Shoulder bag containing digital recorder, a notebook and photograph

I Know What You're Thinking
On table:　　　　　　Drink
Off Stage:　　　　　　Drink

Who's Joe?
On table:　　　　　　Drink
Simon (personal):　Newspaper
Off Stage:　　　　　　Sports bag

Outro

Props as left from previous scenes as appropriate. Note the reference to the photograph can be dropped if 'Mr Critchley, Isn't It?' is omitted from the production.

Furniture List

On stage: Two pub tables with four chairs. The set can be dressed with more pub type furniture at the Director's discretion. The same set is used for all the plays.

Lighting Plot

To open: From black, fade up general lighting

Between scenes: blackout

Sound plot

Cue: *(Tracy tuts to herself, sighs and exits.)* Sound of tripping and glass smashing

www.ingramcontent.com/pod-product-compliance
Lightning Source LLC
Chambersburg PA
CBHW060648030426
42337CB00018B/3503